"My life's footprints"

by
Bozena Helena Mazur-Nowak

© 2019 by the author of this book, Bozena Helena Mazur-Nowak. The book author retains sole copyright to her contributions to this book.

Corrector Editors:
Maureen Clifford - Australia
Per Josefsson - Sweden

Cover, artwork
© Iza Smolarek

Photographs
© Bozena Helena Mazur-Nowak and Iza Smolarek

Edited by Rose Terranova Cirigliano
Published in the US by Rose Books
ISBN-9781088964156 (Independent Publisher)

QUEENS   BROOKLYN   LONDON
ROME   SAN FRANCISCO

To Ian

WITH MANY THANKS

FROM

THE AUTHOR

REIGATE, 09.09.2020

Life's footprints

Life is like a path
Sometimes straight, sometimes curvy
Sometimes you have to climb a hill and
Sometimes you go easily down.
There is a lot of crossroads on the way
It is your choice which one you choose.

You leave footprints behind you.
Sometimes deep, well visible and
Sometimes weak and unseen
What kind of footprints we leave
On Earth, depends only on us.

So do not wait for a miracle
Reach for your dreams gamely
As life is only a one-time bid.

TABLE OF CONTENTS

Life's footprints	**4**
Editor's Introduction *10* by Rose Terranova Cirigliano	
Acknowledgments	*12*
Footprints	*14*
Tangled prose of life	**16**
Autumn without you	**18**
I once had a dream	**19**
Icarus	**21**
I waited so long	**22**
Dies last …	**23**
Telegram	**26**
Pilgrim	**27**
Christmas	**28**
The nest	**29**
The harbor	**31**
Tsunami	**32**
Murdered iris buds	**33**
Ticket to Happiness Station	**34**
Do not ask me to be silent	**35**
How do you say…	**36**
Dilemmas of the Heart	**37**
Mourning Triptych for Kalina….White cliff	**39**
Why?	**40**
The last heartbeat	**41**

All days seem the same	43
Anna and bouquet	44
Dad	45
The woman	47
Summer came again	48
Yesterday	50
Another dawn will come	51
Life is a gift	52
Holes in time	53
Words like a sword	54
Just a moment, please	55
The Source of Love	56
SUNFLOWERS	57
IN A GLASS OF WINE	59
SNAKE	60
I LOVE AUTUMN	61
In a tight weave of the arms	62
Tears in the rain	63
Wind	64
Lost happiness	66
Cormorants will return again	67
The monologue	68
Daddy	70
The stage	71
River	72
My loneliness	73
About the Author	76
Postscript from the Author	80
With Gratitude and Acknowledgement	84

Editor's Introduction

Although English is Bozena Helena's second language, her poetic soul manages to find the right words to conjure the moments captured on paper of her life, her loves, her longings, and her memories. You can smell, and hear, as well as see her world, and the feelings engendered by a life of longing and awareness of the marks we leave along the way of our journey. In **Dilemmas of the Heart** we stand with her in the past fully sensing with her the place and time in her homeland:

> **Dilemmas of the Heart**
>
> Each night I return to those green fields
> To the fragrant linden trees, willows with the outstretched arms
> I count, up there in the sky, storks arriving with the Spring
> And in my mind, I circle around my grandmother's cottage
>
> I listen to the brook babbling in the morning

And to grandfather's violin playing in the evening
I bring my entreaties to the roadside chapel,
To allow the pilgrim to return with a bowed head

Each night, I return from a distant land,
To where you can hear the wonders of Chopin's playing
To the fragrant fields of Mickiewicz's stanzas
'Dabrowski's Mazurka* will remain in the heart

Walk with Bozena down her life's path, and share in the rich memories and moments. Enjoy this wonderful collection of a truly gifted poet.

* Polish anthem

Acknowledgments:

Very special thanks to all my fellow poets from all around the world, who were my first readers and critics.

Thanks to *Rose Terranova Cirigliano*, a great poet, and publisher, who chose my work for many of her anthologies and wrote an introduction to this volume.

Thanks to *Maureen Clifford* (Australia), Per Josefsson (Sweden) correctors.
Thanks to *Iza Smolarek* (UK/Poland) for lovely pictures, which complement my work.
Thanks to *Kathy Figueroa, Delo Isufi, Chris Bodor, John E WordSlinger, Asoke Kumar Mitra, and Aziz Mountassir* for postscripts to this book.

Thanks to all the countless people, who gave me the strength to cope with my disease and encouraged me to keep writing.

Thanks to all readers, who will decide to reach for my book.

Thank you all,
Bozena Helena Mazur-Nowak

FOOTPRINTS

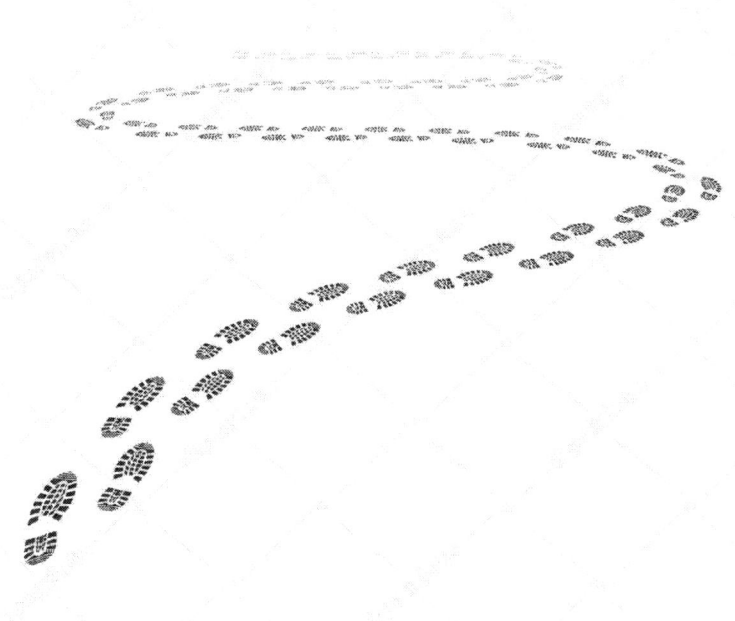

Tangled prose of life

I stand before you my life
You know that all I am is yours
Give me your hand; will be livelier
We go together on rough roads

I no longer know who is whose shadow
You and me I can see
Would not look like our pair
Should always live in harmony

Please help me around the corners
Do not let me fall off the track
Protect my life from intruders,
Plagues and all the difficult choices

On the way through the tangled prose
The tired heart often hurts
Sit down in the shade of the chestnut
Let us soothe the heart with autumn

Autumn without you

The sun is getting lower in the sky
dawn brings darker days and
colder winds conquer the world.

I look for birds migrating south.
One by one they disappear into the distance.
How I would love to go with them.

Like the sun breaking through the leaves
you appear to love me
and yet - like a leaf in a gust of wind
you are gone from me today.

We liked to walk through the park together
holding hands, kicking leaves.
You always loved autumn days
and frolicking in the leaves.

Our bench in the park is empty

I once had a dream

I used to have a dream
Hope was my sister
So much I wanted to live

Believed in everlasting love
And the forgiveness of sins;
I was young and naive, trusting

Now nightmares come at night,
Whispers to me softly.
Dreams blew away with the wind

Autumn of life caught up with me
My heart is so cold already.
Forgotten; what love is

Icarus

all his dreams of returning to Athens
he drew in detail, in his deepest dreams
dressed in bird feathers and wax
took his son, his greatest treasure
and flew high to meet the birds in the sky

young Daedalus delighted with freedom
became deaf to his parent's advice
higher and higher, he rose to the sun
the joy of heart won out over common sense
instead of freedom, painful downfall and death

the old father found his son's body in the sea
and wrapped him with love in a funerary shroud
gave the island his son's name, then flew away
although he never reached his home in Athens,
he regained his freedom, but forever broke his heart

I waited so long

I have been waiting for a miracle
Everyone used to tell me: be strong
Do not show your tears to the world
You will go through the pros and cons

The whole world was sure that I had everything
But I've been waiting for you

I saw a light in the sky,
It blinked at me from above
I didn't believe what I saw
Could it be the Angel of love has given me a sign

Let the rainfall and wash away my tears
Let it fill the soul and drown fears

Out of the darkness spawned a new day
The pain will turn into joy
My weakness is my strength now
In your eyes I'm beautiful

And the joy in my heart and peace
I want to live again

Dies last ...

I write letters to you, my daughter,
Every day a new letter, and perhaps the same
I said in these letters almost everything
And still, so much I have to say,
I love you, you know, do you remember?
I wanted to remind you I'm waiting;
You are still as cold as icicles
And your heart is as hard as a rock, but

I still have hope, thanks to this I'm alive -
Without hope, what is life worth?
Someone once said so beautifully,
That hope dies last

Telegram

every day throughout the world
a woman, wife, girlfriend
waiting for the return of the soldier
sometimes gets an unexpected telegram

Beautiful sunny day
The whole world smells of spring
So you want to live so much

Doorbell

I'm not waiting for anyone
You're so far away
I really like it when you wear a uniform

Telegram
For me?

With trembling hands
I cuddle up to my chest your name

This can not be true!
You promised to come back in May

Sunny Sunday
The world smells so beautiful
And I do not want to live anymore

Pilgrim

The North Star in the sky flickers
Pointing the way for lost hikers
I wonder how many weary pilgrims
Just wandered astray in life

At the crossroads, once again I stand
I asked which way to take my heart
So much pain I carry in my luggage
My love lives only in my mind

Day after day with my sister Hope
I'm looking for answers to make sense
Before time makes me go into oblivion
I want the sun to shine again for me

Christmas

beautiful spruce at neighbor's window
so proud and festooned with a hundred lanterns
they say that the family will arrive in droves
They worry whether enough space for them

and here, it is so quiet, so quiet
I read the yellowed letter's pages
covered with a patina of time

turkey is lazily walking in the garden
and asks for survival

children are looking from frames on the walls
such as small and joyful

trembling hands clinging memories to the heart
a wafer is crying on the plate

The nest

the nest, once-bustling
with the chatter of young chicks
strewn with soft down
fragrant with bird's milk
today is empty

the chicks have grown
flown away into the wide world
built their own nests
and forgot the familiar one

the lonely old mother
resting her head on the nest's edge
gazes into the distance
towards the clouds

the tear in her eye, frozen
her heart pounds with pain
at every shadow in flight
she looks with longing

the nest, once-bustling
today is empty
memories lurk in the corners
but will they fill the emptiness?

the harbor

shouted at the loneliness - go away!
packed his travel bundle
took his faithful dog
and set off into the world far
following his heart

in a foreign land at the end of the world
found a warm home shelter
the harbor a good word and a smile

yesterday he cursed his fate
today he knows that lives again

Tsunami

black coffee bitter as wormwood
maybe sugar lost its sweetness
twisted tale without rhyme or rhythm
between the cup and the touch of lips

ponderous haste sat opposite me
it can not keep up with the flow of thoughts
the world paused, as though in silent hatred
the Tsunami of evil and hypocrisy flooded our world

murdered iris buds

wrapped with love
they were nesting tightly
around a mailbox
and were a great pride

in the night,
the hand of a cruel murderer
broke off the tiny buds
robbed them of life
and took all the joy with them

"now murdered iris remain
in the sunshine as a marker"

shiny tear in the eye
large splinter in the heart
endless sorrow
and the question;
why?

Ticket to Happiness Station

In front of the ticket office,
the queue is long, as usual,
I turn a coin in my hand and wait.
Cashier winks at me amicably.
'Where would you like to go'?

I look around with abashment.
'You are holding up the queue'- someone urges
'Can I have a ticket to Happiness Station, please'?

A blonde standing behind me laughs loudly,
'Would you listen to her! Ha, ha!'

'So what about the ticket'? - the cashier asks again
'Happiness Station, please'-I repeat shyly

This time the lady at the ticket office loses her patience.
'Go have fun somewhere else, lady – she barks at me'
Young boy wearing wire-rimmed glasses looks at me sympathetically,
the only one in the long queue.

I squeeze the coin tightly in my hand and walk away.
I leave the station and walk along the river.
I hear beautiful music coming from a moored barge
I stop for a while to listen to the lovely sounds.
'Happiness must live here'- I think.

I kiss the coin in my hand and throw it in the river for luck.
I will come back here again. For sure, I will.

Do not ask me to be silent

It is difficult to tell the heart: "do not cry"
For that which is buried in its depths
It is difficult not to write that it yearns so
Away from home somewhere in a foreign land

My memories are like icons
For which I care very tenderly
I pull the memories out of my mind
In place of lullabies for my granddaughter

Though my own grandmother is gone, she lives in my heart
She and her cottage on the rushing stream
I remember well that the cottage was blue
A garden full of hollyhocks, snapdragons, and bees

The meadows carpeted with red poppies
Weeds in the crops, with which my grandfather battled
Blue sky, above the white-tailed eagle
And in that meadow, I flew kites

White mare with a soft muzzle
Would place her head gently on my shoulder
And with a childish glance, I'd chase
a young colt romping behind the barn

Perhaps I will never again see that
Which lives deep inside my heart
But I will write of it when longing strikes
And I will draw out of my heart that which is dear to me

So do not ask me anymore, to be silent
Because my heart is so very weary
It must unleash what is hidden at its bottom
So it may be washed with dewy tears

How do you say…

You get a message
For which you have been waiting
It takes your breath away
And your whole world falls apart

This is not what you expected!
Not now, not yet!
You still want to do so much
But now, there isn't time

In your head are spinning thoughts
Those thousands of questions
Should I start new things?
Will I have time to finish them?

Why did my name appear on the list?
Were there definitely no willing others?

You sit in the twilight
The world spins before your eyes
Such a shame to have to go
The spice of life still beckons

But you must say goodbye
And find the right words
To comfort your loved ones
And leave no regrets

But how does one say that?

Dilemmas of the Heart

Each night I return to those green fields
To the fragrant linden trees, willows with the outstretched arms
I count, up there in the sky, storks arriving with the Spring
And in my mind, I circle around my grandmother's cottage

I listen to the brook babbling in the morning
And to grandfather's violin playing in the evening
I bring my entreaties to the roadside chapel,
To allow the pilgrim to return with a bowed head

Each night, I return from a distant land,
To where you can hear the wonders of Chopin's playing
To the fragrant fields of Mickiewicz's stanzas
'Dabrowski's Mazurka* will remain in the heart

And our flag, once blood-soaked
Now flutters proudly in the sun under the blue sky
It will always be a reminder to wandering Poles
Of the reason, our Grandfathers sacrificed their lives

Mourning Triptych for Kalina

White cliff
(*with a dedication to Kalina in heaven*)

A storm of curly hair fell down
on her shoulders
when she, coquettishly smiling,
placed a wreath of wildflowers
on her temples.

That image was frozen in the time frame
of her mother's memory.

She left a farewell letter and
dozens of questions unanswered.
She took with her the joy of life,
faith, and hope

From the height of the white cliff
she chose the sea
as the last view
for her beautiful eyes.

Like a bird struck down in flight
she fell downwards
looking for and so longing for peace.

She was only twenty-two years old.
Just venturing into adulthood.
She was supposed to live.

Why?

wrapped with the pain
frozen on the top of the white cliff
she was seeking with an erroneous vision
of fallen Angels

whether it is that beautiful - she thought -
that pushed you off this cliff?

who will fill the emptiness
in the cradle of mother's arms?

wind wiped off tears from her cheeks
bitter grief choked in the throat

hope for a better tomorrow
was swaying in the distance
on the top of waves

how am I supposed to live without You?
she asked feathery, angelic clouds
how am I supposed to live now?

the unanswered question comes back with the wind

The last heartbeat.

It was a day like any other day
an early Monday afternoon in May –
and she was already dancing with the Angels
as her mother read that farewell letter.

She fell limply from the white cliffs
to the ocean whose waves gently bathed her feet,
their susurration a farewell prayer,
then taking flight she rose,
soaring skyward -
riding the winds with widespread wings
like a white seagull.

The last heartbeat whispered
"Forgive me, Mom
Now I'm happy ".

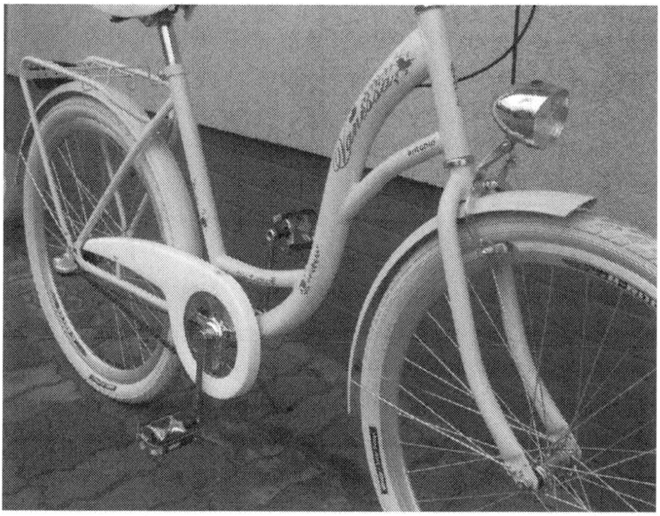

All days seem the same

The outside world is waiting to be healed
but blinds cover the windows
and pain clings like a demon with sharp claws
and the way out is like the Way of the Cross.

On the threshold, the pain stumbles over despair
and in the bedroom guarding memories, curled tightly,
a ginger cat gloomily meows.

There is a void that cannot be filled
when children leave the nest before they are ready to fly.
The nights are darker, all days seem the same.
Unshed tears hover, waiting to fall.
We stare at the blue bike standing orphaned in the hallway
and ask ourselves – why?

Anna and bouquet

Little golden-hair Anna,
with two braided pigtails tied with a red ribbon
and eyes the color of the sky
brought a bouquet to her grandmother
and stared at her.

Standing in front of her grandmother,
twirling the bottom of her dress on her little finger
she said " Mom taught me a poem for you, Grandma
but I forgot it "

Grandma hugged her and sat her on her knees.
Anna sighed with relief,
looked deep into Grandma's eyes,
threw her little arms around Grandma's neck and said:
" Grandma ... I love you the most in all the world ...
after my mommy and daddy "
And as Anna hugged her Grandma tightly,
her Grandma could feel her tiny heart
throbbing against her chest.

Henryk Mazur 1933-2019

Dad

Yesterday you used to lead me through life, holding my hand.
It was you who taught me how to combine letters into words
and showed me how to read with comprehension,
how to find colors in a grey surrounding the world.
You taught me to stand up and fight for myself.

Today I lead you by the hand, like a lost child
and teach you how to pronounce forgotten words.
I try to color your grey, miserable life,
trying to cheer you up when you, helpless, cry.
Today it is me fighting for you, Dad

The woman

It will always defend
you against everything

That's what Mama said
so she squeezed it tightly
until her hand hurt

She whispered a quiet prayer when
they took away her pride and her dignity

She did not fight the
drunken louts

Those raw memories
are helping her
to help others now

Bloodied cross
hangs on her neck

Summer came again

Grandma! Grandma! See, summer came!
Wherever you look, flowers are bowing
their smell braids senses,
intertwines a butterfly into a bouquet
with two bees and a ladybird.

Ah!
I danced in the garden happy and joyful,
I've been giving flowers to you like I used to.
Still, remember how much you loved flowers.
I will put them in a vase next to your photo
I love you, grandma, and I still remember you
And carry you through life, always in my heart.

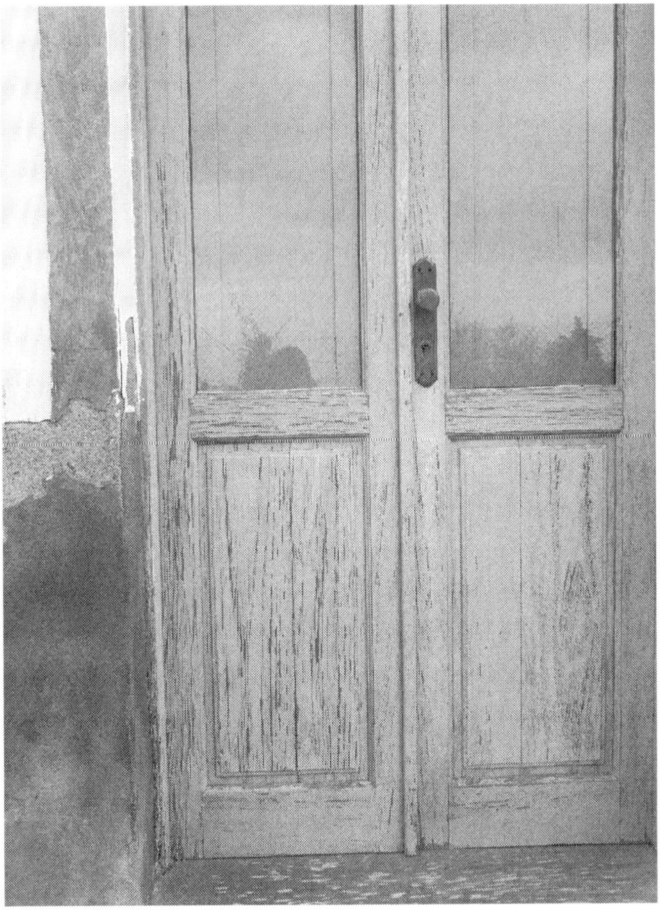

Yesterday

she stood by the window yesterday
and watched as life went by
today flowers wither in pots
she does not squint eyes to the sun anymore

shutters wide open
yellow plaster from the wall crumbles
at the bus stop a gloomy hourglass
says a prayer for her soul

yesterday she greeted with a smile
today adorns memories with tears
she assisted the homeless and hungry
shared a slice of bread with love

she invited pigeons for crumbs
small sparrows squirrels and cats
who will look after a sad group today
which is missing the blue of her eyes

just yesterday she stood by this window ...

another dawn will come

with the arrival of the morning trembling white hands
turn over the pages of the breviary intricately
in silence, spilled letters form words
which will turn into dust when night comes

the setting sun bows to the stars
there is no trace of yesterday's rain
everything that has happened does not matter
anymore
today's tears will also dry up before dawn comes

Life is a gift

He had always a good word for everyone,
although life did not cuddle him.
In his eyes, the sky has already faded slightly
and left its mark on his face.

A wife who once vowed
to not leave him for anything in the world,
has been living in the afterlife for a long time,
and only visits him in dreams now.

Children have traveled around the wide world,
they have their own lives, they do not write, they do not call.
At home, they look at him from the frame on the wall,
so small, helpless, on a walk with his wife.

He often sits on the garden terrace,
and his pockets are stuffed with crumbs.
Feeds hungry local pigeons and sparrows,
he listens to rumors that they bring him in return.

He does not complain, not grumble, not grumble.
He humbly accepts what fate brings
although the fingers are twisted of arthritis,
and the hump grows slowly on his back.
He is still greeted with a smile every single day
like the greatest treasure in his life.

holes in time

the needle pierces the skin
its sting a familiar flavor he tries to forget
but it is so very difficult

"What has happened to me my beloved friend", he asks
everyone I knew has gone a long time ago

you can have this all, a whole kingdom of dirt
but I will always let you down and hurt you like no one else
I wear a crown of shadows and sit on the throne of liars
I cannot do anything

depression makes serious thoughts and feelings all disappear
you are someone else and I am still stuck here
a million miles away, if only I could start over from the beginning
I would go a different way

if I only could to do so ...

words like a sword

we create beauty with words
they are not cliched by time, eternity will not fray their edges
their message shines like a torch in the dark night
the message carries with it its splendor

sometimes words will become a beautiful story
their echo reverberates by breaking the silence
they will reflect with beauty in our souls
giving nice warmth despite the cold around

everything is possible you just need to dream
the pen carries thoughts straight out of the heart and
onto paper
sadly, when we cannot find the words to express ourselves
sometimes, somewhere, someone reaches for the sword

just a moment, please

The aroma of a waiting cup of fragrant coffee
fills the room and tempts me to wake
I do not want to get up,
I want to stay cocooned with your warmth
and your scent which you left on the pillow next to me
I have imprisoned you under my closed eyelids

I feel so good
the curtain in the open window dances
I feel a breeze's finger touch my back
Wild birds are singing loudly
like a mad alarm clock,
brutally bringing me back to reality
it's time to get up
for sparring with the new day

when my friend, night, comes
I will cuddle into your arms again

The Source of Love

At the top of the stairs of your Church,
were scattered crumbs of eternity. Between
them, I found the sweetness of your heart.
You asked me to stay, even though I was unworthy.

You forgave my sins and didn't ask for anything.
Bestowed me with never-ending love.
The memory of your gentle touch,
made me spin with unlimited trust.

You – the enchanting mirage of endless love,
rain down on me like Heavenly brightness.
Stand close by me – stay in my soul and my mind
and deep down in my heart – wherever I am.

SUNFLOWERS

They were pushing
And they were angry at the sky
They wanted to steal
some praise from the sun
And they ended their paradise life
On a carpet of green grass instead

So now they stood and watched with longing
On the extremely long stalks
As if they wanted to touch the sky once more
And the sun, proudly from above,
Now looks down at them

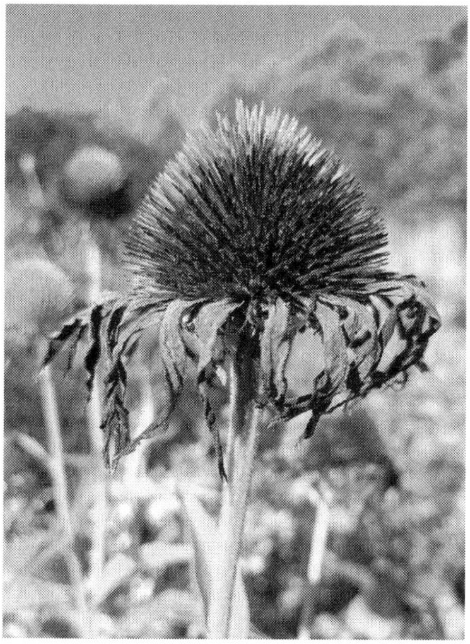

IN A GLASS OF WINE

I'm wondering
between the entrance and the exit
I am looking for you in vain
You have perished
Only our photo on the wall
is still hanging

Here you still look at me
the same way
The moment of happiness
was frozen in that frame
The room is so ominous
at twilight today

You went away and took
the candlelight with you
You cut my dreams into dust
And they blew with the wind
Now, in a glass of wine,
I try to find - the meaning of life

SNAKE

You wrapped yourself around me like a snake.
Directing to my ear hissed spells.
You have bitten me in my neck with your teeth.
And injected into my skin a drop of venom.

I lived flabbily, fainted. Except you,
I no longer saw the world.
You were for me night and day
Were autumn, winter, spring, and summer.

Today only a scar remains me of you.
Two tiny holes on my pale neck.
On my pillow, you left your molting skin.
I am slowly coming back to life.

I LOVE AUTUMN

I love the Indian summer
Clutched to the wind
And leaves carried on their tales
The birds are concerned
Sitting on their suitcases
They are gathering for a journey
overseas - far away

I love Miss Lady Autumn
Clad in purple
And those mists like milk
and hoarfrost at dawn
Grey, heavy clouds
Hanging over our heads
Wellies and umbrellas
Dripping on the porch

I love the pale sun
hanging so low
Affectionately kissing
small heads of Asters
I love absolutely
everything in autumn
Without any grievances or excuses
I just love autumn...

In a tight weave of the arms

Two hearts and the strength of a big bell
They were entwined in the prayer of love
They were inebriated with each other

The world did not exist for them at all
Here at the moment, they were alone on the Earth

Embarrassed, day knocked on the window

The heart of the bell gently sang
In the tight weave of their arms
They were calmly breathing
And the curtain was gently wavy
The pale dawn poured in through the window
And the room still smelled of sin

tears in the rain

pregnant rain clouds
hanging low, you can touch them
I stretch out my hands catching drops

I like to walk in the rain
then no one can see me cry
flits between drops

people hiding under umbrellas
and look at me with surprise
I do not care what they think

Rain gently flushed grief
helps cool down a break
Get me back to life

wind

suddenly fell on me today in the garden
where I sat reading the wonderful verse
the wind in my hair dipped their toes
and my tangled tresses are slashed
then again it gently rubbed my hair

brushed my neck and shoulders flow over
gently slid his hands under my dress
I flushed and embarrassed burned
and I felt like my blood pulsing in my temples

This scatterbrain no thought to give me a break
getting nicer and caressed me flirtatiously

I whispered when he stopped dreamy
come back once more mischievous wind to me

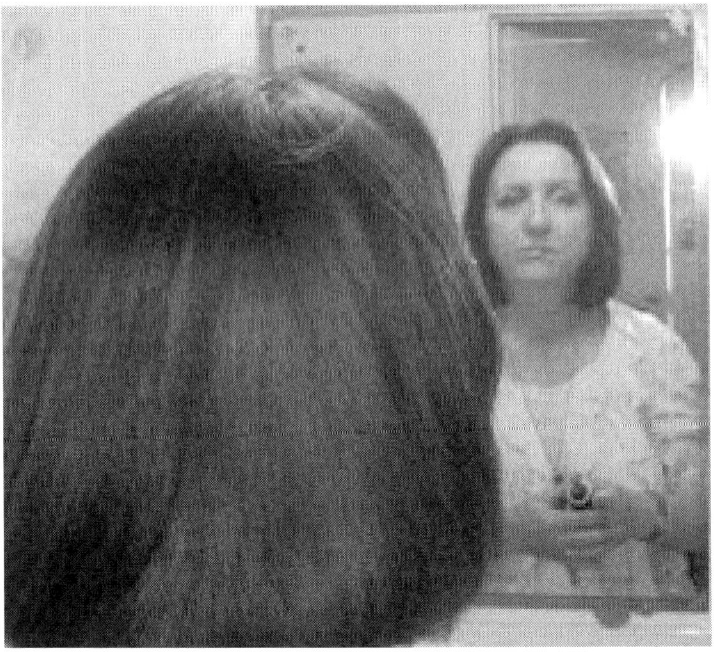

lost happiness

I look at the photograph
a moment of happiness enclosed in a frame
in front of the mirror
I brush my hair with my fingers
silver has been woven into the ebony
my green-gold eyes embraced
by a web of crow's feet
I smile at myself today
but still, remember yesterday.
a tear glistens, ready to flow from the frame
I look at a woman by the mirror
at her pale face
silver is embedded into ebony
and eyes swollen with tears
I wonder where did she lose her happiness

cormorants will return again

cormorants swing in a circle above the beach
looking down at the empty nest
they unite in a V formation ready for a flight overseas
the sand glitters with golden amber
white shells in my clenched palm remind me of
yesterdays.

So much noise - yesterday,
the beach was buzzing, with barely room to move -
now an overturned chaise recalls
sails a-flutter in summer winds
the empty beach has frozen in silent reverie
recalling the sighs of lovers
and the hope that the cormorants will return again

the monologue

the sea does not delight the eyes anymore
and music of foamy waves fades
before it reaches the shore
insanely wild gulls pierce the sky
sun shrunken and sailing boats so empty

the monologue of death on a deserted beach
dead beauty is like yesterday's love
waves in madness chasing after death
I look out of the window on that dance of
destruction

prayer trembles on the purple lips
suffering stuck to the back like a hump
life crumbles us like rotten trees
and severs and scatters our fate like leaves

we are so weak without knowing the future
we play like children with crippled dolls
helpless like a fish out of water
we waste energy fighting with windmills

My beloved father, Henryk Mazur 1933 - 2019

Daddy

A lovely pair of trousers
hanging on the arm of the chair
by the bed, slippers left where you put them
on the armchair, your faithful dog cuddled
into your favorite sweater.

In the drawer an album with yellowed photos.
A bunch of letters from your old love
and a copybook with poems,
your last one written mere days ago.

In the midst of all this, filled with heartache
I hide my face in my hands and ask why you left.

Yesterday you kissed my hands and stroked my hair
I hugged tightly to your heart,
trusting that now it will all be better,
but this morning's phone call ripped my heart in half
and took away my illusions,
took you away too... never to return.

Now, ubiquitous sadness has filled the house you left.
Daddy, I love You and I miss you already so much.

(Reigate, 26 March 2019)

The stage

You come upon the stage
and awkwardly take the first steps.
You learn diction, you play other roles.
For some you get applause - others go unnoticed
only the sufferer's booth is empty
No one will help you when you forget your lines,
you have to improvise; there is no understudy.

Failure is painful. No action can be repeated.
You always know that too late.

Someday you will fall asleep
and not wake up again,
that will be the last act of your role
and only the future will show
if a poster with your name
would be kept on the wall for posterity.

Only time will tell your truth.

River

it flows out from the source of life
lazily and calmly - a shallow stream
that can change in a moment into a rapid brook
flowing over and around obstacles
despite cutting corners, becoming wider,
it still flows ahead.
sometimes breaking its banks
and flooding into the meadows of everyday life.
Searching for the escape it creates new channels
giving rise to new rivers that trickle
into a valley of golden autumn
flowing lazily, slowly meandering, slowly
heading for the sea of disappearance

our life

my loneliness

she clings to me like a bur
That one day accidentally fell on me.
she took me firmly under my arm,
came home and stayed here for good

she reads the morning papers with me
and writes letters to herself
wears my trodden slippers
and knows what I do not

when I leave, she waits humbly
does not complain, is not grouchy;
she is happy when I come back
and opens the door for me

she says to me: you are not alone
I live with you, no matter what
I love you and I will stay forever
I will always be close as your skin

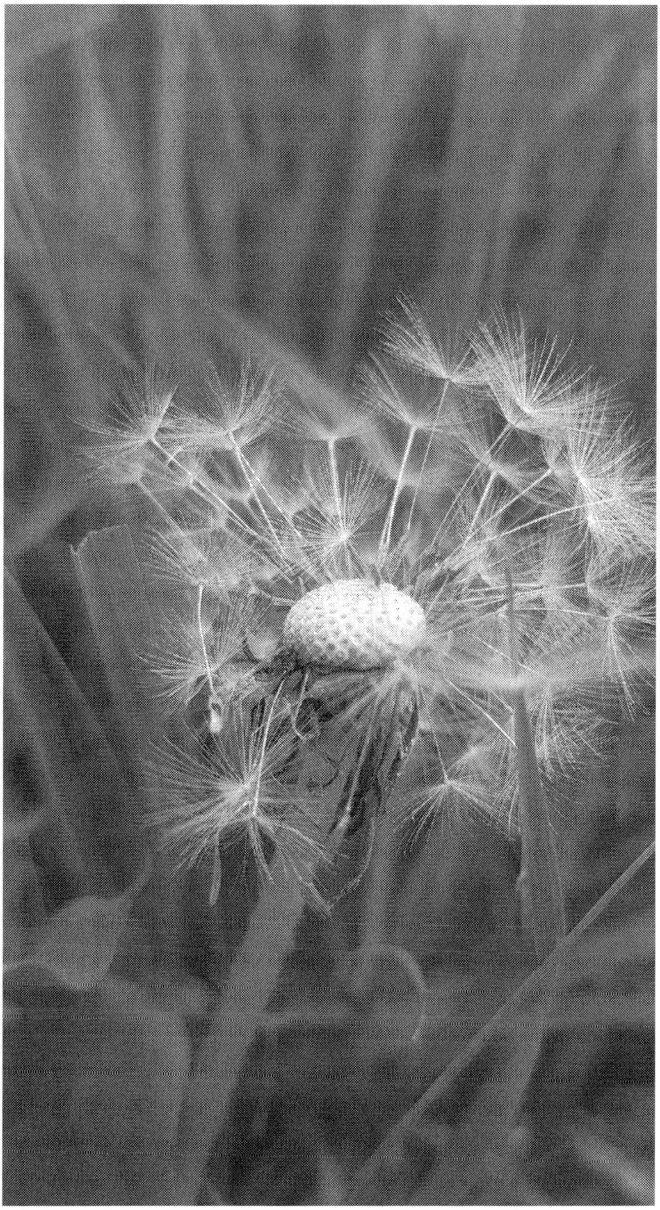

About the Author

Bozena Helena Mazur-Nowak was born in Opole, Poland. In 2004 in search of work migrated to Great Britain, where she lives. Emigration was a difficult choice for her because, as she says, "Life in the home country on the edge of poverty, with no chance to work. Miserable existence leading almost to madness, and suddenly opens a window to the world and invites you to reach for new possibilities. So I reach – not without fear, after a long deliberation – " I reach and leaving the past behind begin to build a new life. At the heart is a longing that brings poems".

She published six volumes of poetry; four in Polish and two in English. She also writes prose and released a novel and a few short story collections.

Her work may be found in numerous worldwide anthologies and magazines.
Winner of many poetry competitions.

Proud holder of many diplomas, awards, and distinctions.
- 2015 Maria Konopnicka award for her merits to the Polish culture.
- 2015 Tadeusz Micinski Expressionist Award

- 2015 St Moniuszko's Gold Statuette was awarded by her in Vilnius, for allegiance to Polish culture in her work, and its dissemination worldwide.
- 2017 Literary Award of Klemens Janicki
- 2017 A distinction for her novel "Blue cottage" seat as a child-friendly book.

Bozena has worked very hard at doing just that and her poetry is now read in many poetry journals and publications around the world.

Member of Union of Polish Writer's Abroad (since 1946), Polish Authors' Association, and the Association of American Poets. Her poetry was translated into Franch, Spanish, Swedish, Russian, Arabic, Telugu languages.

She is also a translator to fellow poets, translates from and into English.

Postscript from the Author

It is so difficult to describe in just a few words what pushes us to write. As far as I can remember, poetry has always been a part of me. I remember my family home was filled with poetry: full of books, full of people. My mom was a great singer and dancer. Dad used to play accordion and sing. I still have my dad's diary full of his poems - wonderful love poems for Emily, his last love. I published them in my third book: "At the departure bridge". My father passed away this year and thanks to that he still lives in his poetry.

Our family home was literally drowning in books. My father was capable of spending his last penny on books. He taught me how to read and understand.

My grandparents especially the two grandmothers Maria and Helena passed on to me the family secrets in their endless stories. Grandmother maria taught me how to look with the heart and how to forgive.

I entered adulthood in a company of wonderful poets such as Galczynski, Tuwim, and Pawlikowska-Jasnorzewska. During difficult times in my life the world of poetry - me secret world has helped me to survive.

In 2004 I decided to immigrate to the UK. It was a difficult decision for me, fueled by a life in the home country, on the edge of poverty, and with no chance to work, which was elementary frustrating, especially after looking through a window onto the world that was created by Poland joining the Europian Union.

Longing for the country of my childhood intensified my writing. It took several years to show my writing to the world. In 2013 I released my first full-length volume of poems in English "Whispered". A year later I put in a readers hands second one "Blue Longing".
2014 and 2015 I wrote a novel a few short story collections. And now the time comes for a new poetry volume "Footprints of my life".
The Internet gives me many opportunities to forge new friendships, and get to know new people. It promotes the exchange of experience. It helps in learning new things. As a result, I have met a number of wonderful poets from all over the world.
And I am happy to have met you, my readers.

I hope that my poems stir your thoughts, inspire your reflections and leave warmth in your hearts.

Bozena Helena Mazur-Nowak
Poetess with Polish Origin

WITH GRATITUDE AND ACKNOWLEDGEMENT

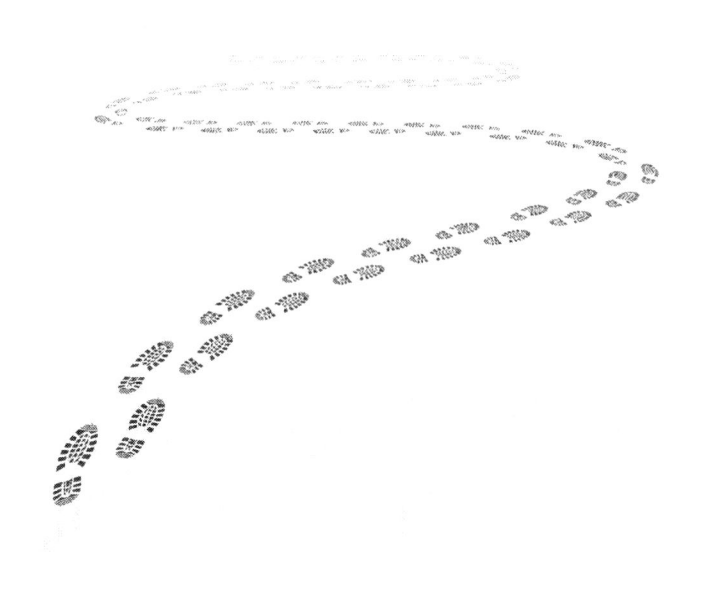

Every time I read poems by Bozena Helena Mazur-Nowak I am inspired to write about her work. I am not a critic, but she has won my recognition for her literary production. Her magnificent qualities shine as I see her poetry penetrating the depths of the soul.

Bozena Helena glows in the glare of the world with every poem, with each image, and a difference between vision and vision, flirting with the spaces of revelation from inside the experience, not with the pain. Her writing has emerged from the tunnel of silence to declare that women are able to lead and innovate and Bozena Helena has lived in the poem and dwelt in it, remained faithful to its glow, looking for the unique pulse and flow, wiping off its ugliness and deformity. I put myself in a beautiful dilemma, trapped between the harmlessness and toxicity of the poetic scene.

This woman is flying towards an open and ambitious horizon, in a growing and evolving dynamic. However, the most important characteristic is her ability to abandon the feminine self, whilst grasping the rigors of daily life and problems, without losing sight of reality.

Aziz Mountassir,

poet from Casablanca, Morocco

Bozena Helena Mazur-Nowak is a Polish poet with rare dexterity in her use of words and expresses exalted thoughts and emotions with economy of words. Having gone through some poems of Bozena Helena, it has become obvious to me that she is truly a born-poet and she knows how to use words to make a perfect poem.

Her poems represent the human conscience, which is always influenced by God. It is influenced by the good and evil instincts of human mind and nostalgia of joyful days. Her poems describe the beauty of Nature, the philosophy and practical experiences of life. Sparkling combination of words, brevity in expression and abstract ideas made Bozena's poems more beautiful. Her poetry is charged with both passion and power. Her poetry is full of exquisite sensibility with skillful ability and refined emotions.

What she wrote in "TANGLED PROSE OF LIFE",
> I Stand before you my life, You know that all I'm yours, Give me your hand, Will be livelier, We go together on rough roads...-

shows a way to happiness despite difficulties.
> In "THE WOMAN"- she says" It will always defend you against everything "...it never fades away with time.

In " LIFE IS A GIFT"-She wrote-
> "A wife who once vowed, Do not leave him for anything in the world, Has been living in the afterlife for a long time, And only visits him in dreams now"-

depicts a great philosophical insight of life.
Gamut of emotions, cheerful optimism and romantic feel will stay long in the memory of readers.

Aroma of words will open a new window in closed eyelids.

Asoke Kumar Mitra, poet, retired journalist And Editor, Kolkata, INDIA

Drawn out by her heart and to your heart, Bozena Helena Mazur-Nowak and her Poetry stops your body in motion while your mind takes flight. While reading your heart widens, and deepens all of your perceptions, weaving life's realities and fantasies, furthermore her Poetry engages your own memories to live again that has been locked away in your lifes' cherished chamber of remembrance.

You are there with understanding and wisdom, realizing how precious life be. Then, now, and tomorrow...

_John E. WordSlinger

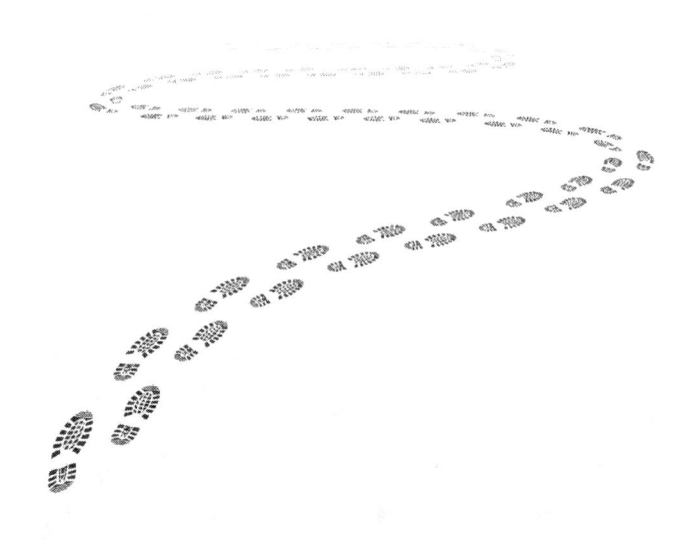

Bozena Helena Mazur-Nowak will lead you on a journey of rough roads with her latest volume of poetry. The poems in "My Life's Footprints" touch on the themes of nature and nurture. Her observations will transport you to Happiness Station, where dreams fly away with the wind, tears cascade from pregnant rain clouds, and suitcases are stuffed with heartache. These pages are filled with joy and sadness. Ultimately, the poet's well-crafted words speak of the promise of hope. Like life, this uplifting collection is a genuine gift.

-Chris Bodor

Founding member of the Ancient City Poets

While reading Bozean Helena Mazur-Nowak's poems, it looks like all the world's flowers have turned into letters and knitted rainbows in the marvelous sky of her book. Her poems bring the smell of roses, the waves of the sea, the stars look like they're swimming and dancing in the vast thought ocean of the poetess. In her poems you can find love for life, love for humanity, love, for nature. Her verses soar with majesty and elegance in this book. Maybe her origin, maybe the place she lives in, her education or her friends, have caused the poetess to have such a great soul. While reading her book, you find yourself in a world as much real, as surreal. Right there, in her verses, nature becomes one with the reader. Her soul's beauty flourishes in all of four seasons. This book is the poetess Bozena Helena Mazur-Nowak herself. I wish her a good journey for future books.

With consideration,
Colonel pilot, lawyer and poet
Delo Isufi
Tirana, Albania

The predominant themes in Bozena Helena Mazur-Nowak's latest collection of poetry, "My life's footprints," are longing, loss, and remembrance. Her work is infused with a sadness which is probably shared by many immigrants immersed in a new culture, as they miss the people, places, and way of life that were, often of necessity, left behind.

This geographical distance, however, can be somewhat bridged by the power of writing about cherished memories. This is exemplified by the following excerpt from Bozena's poem,

> "Do not ask me to be silent":
>
> Perhaps I will never again see that
>
> Which lives deep inside my heart
>
> But I will write of it when longing strikes
>
> And I will draw out of my heart that which is dear to me

Loss also figures sharply and nowhere is this more achingly apparent than in her poem, "Daddy," written the day her dearly loved father passed on. She also grieves the suicide of a young woman, in "Mourning Triptych for Kalina." This is not a light-hearted collection but, rather, one that fearlessly plumbs the depths of sorrow.

Remembrance brings moments of joy, as childhood memories of sights, sounds, and the fragrances of spring and summer, at her grandmother's cottage, lift her spirits.

I don't recall where I first became acquainted with Bozena's work. It might've been when we were both contributors to the Australia Times Poetry Magazine, many years ago, or, possibly, via social media. Regardless, I've been reading her poetry for a considerable period of time and am impressed by her sensitivity, candor, and dedication. She writes prolifically and fearlessly. I hope her journey through the realm of literature brings her well-deserved happiness and success!

***Kathy Figueroa

BIOGRAPHIES

MAUREEN CLIFFORD

A poet and author, a mother to one son, and over the years numerous dearly loved dogs. This self-confessed animal lover lives with her dog Khamah-D Blue in a semi-rural city an hour out of Brisbane.

After 30 years spent in the Private Health Insurance industry a foray for 6 years as a self-employed grazier on a sheep property in SE Queensland was probably the happiest time of my life, and is sadly missed. It certainly got my poetic juices sparking that's for sure.

I held the position of one of the community editors on the now-defunct ABC POOL site for 3 years, and the Editor of the new defunct The Australia Times Poetry Magazine for 4 years, http://www.theaustraliatimes.com.au/ which I greatly enjoyed, but moving on these days sees me as an active on-line member of The Australian Bush Poets Association (ABPA), and the moderator for the Australian Rhyming Poets Facebook page. https://www.facebook.com/AustralianRhymingPoets/

Per Josefsson

Per Josefsson is a swedish literature critic, writer and poet. He is a translator in English and Swedish and has long experience in translating both poetry and prose for several poets and writers.

He is both a language teacher in English and Swedish and has studied at the Swedish university of Graphics and Fine Arts and work daily as an illustrator, graphic designer and artist.

He is married to poet, writer and artist Joanna Svensson Josefsson. They live in an old Shakespeare-like farm from the late 18th century, together with over 8 000 old books and a black cat and surrounded by beautiful nature and wild animals passing thru their huge garden.

A great place for inspiration but also close to cultural life in Lund, Copenhagen and the European continent.

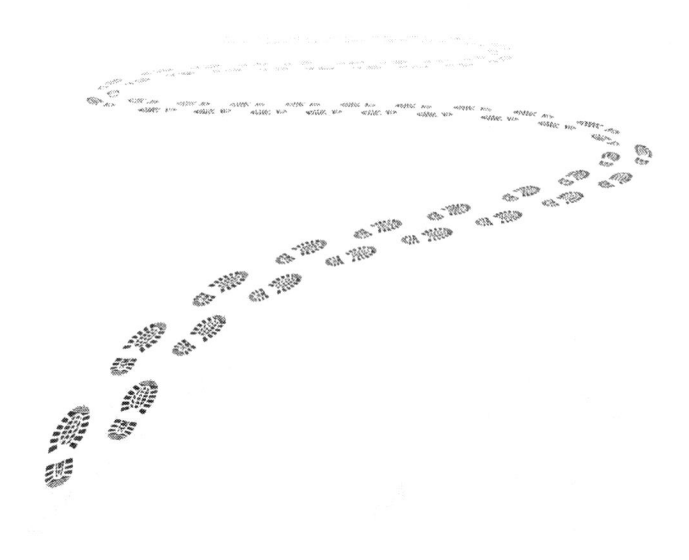

ASOKE KUMAR MITRA

Born 1950, from Kolkata, India, studied at Hindu school and St. Xavier's College, Kolkata.

He is a retired journalist and was editor of "CALCUTTA CANVAS" and "INDUS CHRONICLE".

He is a bilingual poet. He has contributed to various anthologies published in India and abroad. His poems are translated into Hindi, Punjabi, Italian, French, German, Polish, Persian, Arabic, Hebrew, Malay, Mandarin, Romanian, Spanish, Azerbaijani, Russian, Uzbek, Kirghiz, Greek, Swedish, Chinese, Catalan.

"SAVAGE WIND" is his first poetry book, published form Kolkata, India, a bilingual edition, translated into Spanish by Mexican poet Josep Juarez.

Poetry, photography, paintings are his passions.

John E. WordSlinger

Poetry Train
http://www.poetrytrain.com

Memoir-Memoir.com
https://memoir-memoir.com/

Amazon Author Page:
https://www.amazon.com/Mr-John-E-WordSlinger/e/B01AF3E55M
-
https://www.goodreads.com/author/show/4642186.John_E_Wordslinger

Blog:
https://johnewordslinger.wordpress.com
https://speakofthepoetandthepoem.wordpress.com/
https://en.gravatar.com/johnewordslinger

Channel:
https://www.youtube.com/channel/UC-_hrXVNAl-4EI4OUV8ypyA

Music: Begets of Autumn
https://www.youtube.com/channel/UCqmFXYPnztKjNeiXB-ecwVA

Chris Bodor

Chris Bodor is a US poet, who was born in 1967 in Connecticut to an English mother and a Hungarian father. After working for ten years in New York City, he relocated to Florida in 2003.

Six years later, Chris started hosting monthly poetry readings on the last Sunday of every month in St. Augustine, Florida. A YouTube channel was created for the group, known as the Ancient City Poets, in 2018.

During the past 20 years Bodor's poems have appeared in many independent press publications, such as the Lummox Journal, FM Quarterly, and Old City Life.

He is the owner of Poet Plant Press and the Editor-In-Chief of the international literary journal A.C. PAPA (which stands of Ancient City Poets, Authors, Photographers, and Artist).

Delo Isufi

Delo Isufi, he has to his credit, seven poetry collections, one novel and many cycles of poems, has translated many poems from English, French, Russian into the Albanian language. He completed his studies in the Air Force Academy as a pilot. He graduated from the Law Faculty of the TiranaUniversity, Albania. He has several flying hours on a supersonic military jet MiG-19 under every weather condition and held the rank Colonel. He was a lecturer and professor at the aviation academy. As Lawyer, he has been the general Advocate of the Albania StateAdvocacy. Currently, he lives in Tirana, Albania. Now he is a private lawyer.

Kathy Figueroa

Kathy Figueroa is a Canadian poet, photographer, and indie publisher who resides in the beautiful town of Bancroft, in the northern part of Hastings County, Ontario, Canada. The Internet reaches all parts of the globe and, as a result, so do Kathy's often funny and irreverent poems - though some evince a more serious tone. Her versified views of the world can also be found in numerous "hard copy" publications, like newspapers, magazines, dozens of anthologies, and her five published collections: Paudash Poems, Flowertopia, The Cathedral of the Eternal Blue Sky, The Ballad of the PoeTrain Poeteer: Winnipeg to Vancouver, and The Renaissance of Rhyme. In addition, her short play, "Conflicted About The Wolf," was staged in Bancroft, in 2012.

To date, she's created four large literary events, including two "The Word Is Wild Literary Festivals," with another one planned for October, 2019. For many years, Kathy was also involved with various aspects of film production, and, for two years, was

Poetry Editor of the Quinte Arts Council publication, "Umbrella." In 2018, she registered a small press, "Flowertopia Studio," which publishes the work of Canadian poets.

Rose Terranova Cirigliano

Rose Terranova Cirigliano began her writing career in television when she wrote, produced and hosted her own educational television series for the Catholic Television Network of Brooklyn and Queens. In the course of developing educational media she wrote scripts and production notes as well as teacher's manuals for the programs. She is enjoying her early retirement from teaching by writing essays, and memoirs. She established ROSEBOOKS after Lewis Crystal passed away, and has tried to continue his legacy.

Rose grew up in Brooklyn, but has lived most of her life in Queens. She currently lives in Maspeth, NY with her husband Joe, a fellow artist and licensed locksmith, with their dog, "Max".

Iza Smolarek

Iza Smolarek – born 1977. Poet, writer, journalist, cultural activist. Winner of Ministry of Culture and National Heritage bursary (category – literature). Author of the volume "i laze" (Wydawnictwo Portret 2006r.) and "sensory states" (Liberum Arbitrium 2007r.), as well as several crime novels. Winner of numerous literary competitions. Nominated for the Dżonka Literary Prize in the most talented young Polish poets category (2007). Translated into Ukrainian and English. From Poznan, currently living and working in London.

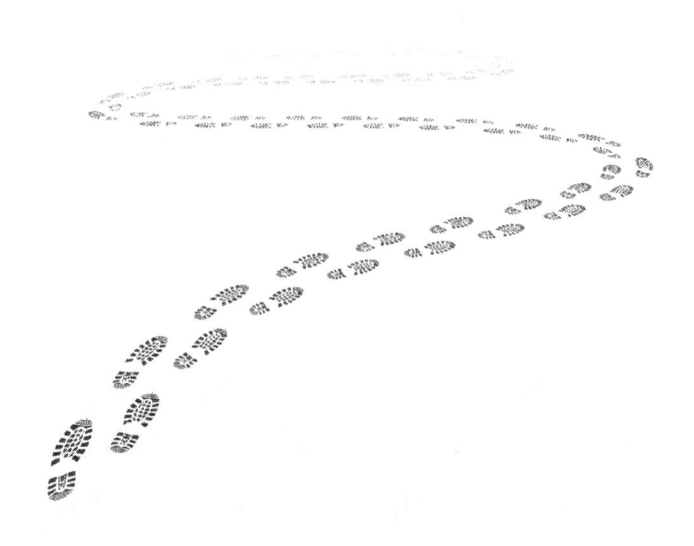

Other Books by the Author

Doom: A Short Story Collection
by Bozena Helena Mazur-Nowak | Nov 12, 2015

Interrupted Life: A Short Story Collection
by Bozena Helena Mazur-Nowak, Rose Terranova Cirigliano, ed | May 20, 2016

Printed in Great Britain
by Amazon